Journey From the Ashes

Journal

Erica Gumieny

ISBN: 979-8-9931562-2-4

Welcome to the Journey from the Ashes Journal

This journal, created as a companion for the Journey from the Ashes devotional, is a space to help you reflect more deeply on the daily insights within each month's theme.

Use these pages to write your thoughts, intentions, prayers, and reflections as you walk through your journey day by day.

At the end of each month, you'll be invited to let go of what no longer serves you—tearing out those pages as a symbol of freedom—and then write a new declaration rooted in His truth and love.

Let this be a safe place to be honest—with yourself and with God—about what you're learning, feeling, releasing, and receiving along the way.

My prayer is that you will look back at the end of this journey—you'll stand in awe and say, "Wow... look at what God did!"

JANUARY

Enough

January - Enough

Prayerful Intentions

As I begin this path on my journey, I pray that:

_____

_____

_____

_____

_____

_____

_____

_____

_____

_____

_____

_____

_____

_____

_____

_____

_____

January - Enough
Daily Notes

January - Enough

Daily Notes

January - Enough
Daily Notes

January - Enough

January - Enough
Daily Notes

January - Enough

Monthly Reflection

How did this theme of Enough show up in my life this month?

_____
_____
_____
_____
_____
_____

What did God reveal to me about His love?

_____
_____
_____
_____
_____
_____

How can I show myself or others compassion?

_____
_____
_____
_____
_____
_____

Where can God guide me in this area moving forward?

_____
_____
_____
_____
_____
_____

January - Enough

January - Enough

Monthly Release

What lies are you ready to stop believing? Write them down here, rip this page out, and GET RID OF THEM!

_____

_____

_____

_____

_____

_____

_____

_____

_____

_____

_____

_____

January - Enough

January - Enough

Monthly Declaration

What did the truth of God's word reveal to you?

_____
_____
_____
_____
_____

What scriptures spoke to you the most?

_____
_____
_____
_____
_____

What forgiveness can you give or receive?

_____
_____
_____
_____
_____

What is your prayer as we finish this path?

_____
_____
_____
_____
_____

FEBRUARY

Loved

February - Loved

Prayerful Intentions

As I begin this path on my journey, I pray that:

_____

_____

_____

_____

_____

_____

_____

_____

_____

_____

_____

_____

_____

_____

_____

_____

_____

_____

_____

_____

February- Loved
Daily Notes

February- Loved

February- Loved
Daily Notes

_____

_____

_____

_____

_____

_____

_____

_____

_____

_____

_____

_____

_____

_____

_____

_____

_____

_____

_____

_____

_____

_____

_____

_____

February- Loved

Daily Notes

February- Loved
Daily Notes

February - Loved

Monthly Reflection

How did this theme of Loved show up in my life this month?

_____
_____
_____
_____
_____
_____

What did God reveal to me about His love?

_____
_____
_____
_____
_____
_____

How can I show myself or others compassion?

_____
_____
_____
_____
_____
_____

Where can God guide me in this area moving forward?

_____
_____
_____
_____
_____
_____

February- Loved

February - Loved

Monthly Release

What lies are you ready to stop believing? Write them down here, rip this page out, and GET RID OF THEM!

February- Loved

February- Loved

Monthly Declaration

What did the truth of God's word reveal to you?

_____
_____
_____
_____
_____

What scriptures spoke to you the most?

_____
_____
_____
_____
_____
_____

What forgiveness can you give or receive?

_____
_____
_____
_____
_____

What is your prayer as we finish this path?

_____
_____
_____
_____
_____

MARCH

Forgiven

March - Forgiven

Prayerful Intentions

As I begin this path on my journey, I pray that:

_____

_____

_____

_____

_____

_____

_____

_____

_____

_____

_____

_____

_____

_____

_____

_____

_____

_____

March - Forgiven

March - Forgiven

March - Forgiven
Daily Notes

March - Forgiven

March - Forgiven

Daily Notes

March - Forgiven

Monthly Reflection

How did this theme of Forgiven show up in my life this month?

_____
_____
_____
_____
_____
_____

What did God reveal to me about His love?

_____
_____
_____
_____
_____

How can I show myself or others compassion?

_____
_____
_____
_____
_____

Where can God guide me in this area moving forward?

_____
_____
_____
_____
_____

March - Forgiven

March - Forgiven

Monthly Release

What lies are you ready to stop believing? Write them down here, rip this page out, and GET RID OF THEM!

March - Forgiven

March - Forgiven

Monthly Declaration

What did the truth of God's word reveal to you?

_____
_____
_____
_____
_____
_____

What scriptures spoke to you the most?

_____
_____
_____
_____
_____
_____

What forgiveness can you give or receive?

_____
_____
_____
_____
_____
_____

What is your prayer this month?

_____
_____
_____
_____
_____
_____

APRIL

Wanted

April - Wanted

Prayerful Intentions

As I begin this path on my journey, I pray that:

_____

_____

_____

_____

_____

_____

_____

_____

_____

_____

_____

_____

_____

_____

_____

_____

_____

_____

_____

_____

April - Wanted

Daily Notes

April - Wanted

April - Wanted
Daily Notes

April - Wanted

April - Wanted
Monthly Reflection

How did this theme of Wanted show up in my life this month?

_____
_____
_____
_____
_____
_____

What did God reveal to me about His love?

_____
_____
_____
_____
_____
_____

How can I show myself or others compassion?

_____
_____
_____
_____
_____
_____

Where can God guide me in this area moving forward?

_____
_____
_____
_____
_____

April - Wanted

Monthly Release

What lies are you ready to stop believing? Write them down here rip this page out and GET RID OF THEM!

April - Wanted

April - Wanted

Monthly Declaration

What did the truth of God's word reveal to you?

_____
_____
_____
_____
_____

What scriptures spoke to you the most?

_____
_____
_____
_____
_____

What forgiveness can you give or receive?

_____
_____
_____
_____
_____

What is your prayer this month?

_____
_____
_____
_____
_____

MAY

Found

May - Found

Prayerful Intentions

As I begin this path on my journey, I pray that:

_____

_____

_____

_____

_____

_____

_____

_____

_____

_____

_____

_____

_____

_____

_____

_____

_____

_____

_____

May - Found

May - Found

May - Found
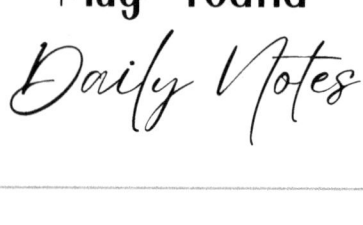
Daily Notes

May - Found
Daily Notes

May - Found
Daily Notes

May - Found
Monthly Reflection

How did this theme of Found show up in my life this month?

_____
_____
_____
_____
_____
_____

What did God reveal to me about His love?

_____
_____
_____
_____
_____
_____

How can I show myself or others compassion?

_____
_____
_____
_____
_____
_____

Where can God guide me in this area moving forward?

_____
_____
_____
_____
_____
_____

May - Found

May - Found
Monthly Release

What lies are you ready to stop believing? Write them down here, rip this page out, and GET RID OF THEM!

May - Found

May - Found

Monthly Declaration

What did the truth of God's word reveal to you?
_____
_____
_____
_____
_____

What scriptures spoke to you the most?
_____
_____
_____
_____
_____

What forgiveness can you give or receive?
_____
_____
_____
_____
_____

What is your prayer this month?
_____
_____
_____
_____
_____

JUNE

Repurposed

June - Repurposed

Prayerful Intentions

As I begin this path on my journey, I pray that:

_____

_____

_____

_____

_____

_____

_____

_____

_____

_____

_____

_____

_____

_____

_____

_____

_____

June - Repurposed
Daily Notes

June - Repurposed
Daily Notes

June - Repurposed
Daily Notes

June - Repurposed
Daily Notes

June - Repurposed
Daily Notes

June - Repurposed

Monthly Reflection

How did this theme of Repurposed show up in my life this month?

_____
_____
_____
_____
_____
_____

What did God reveal to me about His love?

_____
_____
_____
_____
_____
_____

How can I show myself or others compassion?

_____
_____
_____
_____
_____
_____

Where can God guide me in this area moving forward?

_____
_____
_____
_____
_____
_____

June - Repurposed

June - Repurposed

Monthly Release

What lies are you ready to stop believing? Write them
down here, rip this page out, and GET RID OF THEM!

June - Repurposed

June - Repurposed

Monthly Declaration

What did the truth of God's word reveal to you?

_____
_____
_____
_____
_____
_____

What scriptures spoke to you the most?

_____
_____
_____
_____
_____
_____

What forgiveness can you give or receive?

_____
_____
_____
_____
_____
_____

What is your prayer this month?

_____
_____
_____
_____
_____
_____

JULY

Free

July - Free

Prayerful Intentions

As I begin this path on my journey, I pray that:

_____

_____

_____

_____

_____

_____

_____

_____

_____

_____

_____

_____

_____

_____

_____

_____

_____

_____

July - Free
Daily Notes

July - Free
Daily Notes

July - Free
Daily Notes

July - Free
Daily Notes

July - Free
Daily Notes

July - Free
Monthly Reflection

How did this theme of Free show up in my life this month?

_____
_____
_____
_____
_____
_____

What did God reveal to me about His love?

_____
_____
_____
_____
_____
_____

How can I show myself or others compassion?

_____
_____
_____
_____
_____
_____

Where can God guide me in this area moving forward?

_____
_____
_____
_____
_____
_____

July – Free

July - Free

Monthly Release

What lies are you ready to stop believing? Write them down here, rip this page out, and GET RID OF THEM!

July - Free

July - Free
Monthly Declaration

What did the truth of God's word reveal to you?

_____
_____
_____
_____
_____
_____

What scriptures spoke to you the most?

_____
_____
_____
_____
_____
_____

What forgiveness can you give or receive?

_____
_____
_____
_____
_____
_____

What is your prayer this month?

_____
_____
_____
_____
_____
_____

AUGUST

Worthy

August - Worthy

Prayerful Intentions

As I begin this path on my journey, I pray that:

_____

_____

_____

_____

_____

_____

_____

_____

_____

_____

_____

_____

_____

_____

_____

_____

_____

_____

_____

_____

_____

_____

August - Worthy
Daily Notes

August - Worthy
Daily Notes

August - Worthy
Daily Notes

August - Worthy

August - Worthy
Monthly Reflection

How did this theme of Worthy show up in my life this month?

_____
_____
_____
_____
_____
_____

What did God reveal to me about His love?

_____
_____
_____
_____
_____
_____

How can I show myself or others compassion?

_____
_____
_____
_____
_____
_____

Where can God guide me in this area moving forward?

_____
_____
_____
_____
_____
_____

August - Worthy

Monthly Release

What lies are you ready to stop believing? Write them
down here, rip this page out, and GET RID OF THEM!

August - Worthy

August - Worthy

Monthly Declaration

What did the truth of God's word reveal to you?

_____
_____
_____
_____
_____
_____

What scriptures spoke to you the most?

_____
_____
_____
_____
_____
_____

What forgiveness can you give or receive?

_____
_____
_____
_____
_____

What is your prayer this month?

_____
_____
_____
_____
_____

SEPTEMBER

Protected

September - Protected

Prayerful Intentions

As I begin this path on my journey, I pray that:

_____

_____

_____

_____

_____

_____

_____

_____

_____

_____

_____

_____

_____

_____

_____

_____

_____

_____

_____

_____

September - Protected
Daily Notes

September - Protected
Daily Notes

September - Protected

Daily Notes

September - Protected
Daily Notes

September - Protected
Daily Notes

September - Protected

Monthly Reflection

How did this theme of Protected show up in my life this month?

_____
_____
_____
_____
_____
_____

What did God reveal to me about His love?

_____
_____
_____
_____
_____

How can I show myself or others compassion?

_____
_____
_____
_____
_____

Where can God guide me in this area moving forward?

_____
_____
_____
_____
_____

September - Protected

September - Protected

Monthly Release

What lies are you ready to stop believing? Write them down here, rip this page out, and GET RID OF THEM!

_____

_____

_____

_____

_____

_____

_____

_____

_____

_____

_____

_____

September - Protected

September - Protected

Monthly Declaration

What did the truth of God's word reveal to you?

_____
_____
_____
_____
_____
_____

What scriptures spoke to you the most?

_____
_____
_____
_____
_____
_____

What forgiveness can you give or receive?

_____
_____
_____
_____
_____
_____

What is your prayer this month?

_____
_____
_____
_____
_____
_____

OCTOBER

Redeemed

October - Redeemed

Prayerful Intentions

As I begin this path on my journey, I pray that:

_____

_____

_____

_____

_____

_____

_____

_____

_____

_____

_____

_____

_____

_____

_____

_____

_____

_____

_____

October - Redeemed
Daily Notes

October - Redeemed
Daily Notes

October - Redeemed
Daily Notes

October - Redeemed

Daily Notes

October - Redeemed
Daily Notes

October - Redeemed

Monthly Reflection

How did this theme of Redeemed show up in my life this month?

_____
_____
_____
_____
_____
_____

What did God reveal to me about His love?

_____
_____
_____
_____
_____
_____

How can I show myself or others compassion?

_____
_____
_____
_____
_____
_____

Where can God guide me in this area moving forward?

_____
_____
_____
_____
_____
_____

October - Redeemed

October – Redeemed

Monthly Release

What lies are you ready to stop believing? Write them down here, rip this page, out and GET RID OF THEM!

October - Redeemed

October - Redeemed

Monthly Declaration

What did the truth of God's word reveal to you?

_____
_____
_____
_____
_____
_____

What scriptures spoke to you the most?

_____
_____
_____
_____
_____
_____

What forgiveness can you give or receive?

_____
_____
_____
_____
_____
_____

What is your prayer this month?

_____
_____
_____
_____
_____
_____

NOVEMBER

Grateful

November - Grateful

Prayerful Intentions

As I begin this path on my journey, I pray that:

_____

_____

_____

_____

_____

_____

_____

_____

_____

_____

_____

_____

_____

_____

_____

_____

_____

_____

_____

November - Grateful

November - Grateful

Daily Notes

November - Grateful

November - Grateful
Daily Notes

November - Grateful

_____
_____
_____
_____
_____
_____
_____
_____
_____
_____
_____
_____
_____
_____
_____
_____
_____
_____
_____
_____
_____
_____
_____
_____
_____
_____
_____
_____

October - Grateful

Monthly Reflection

How did this theme of Grateful show up in my life this month?

_____
_____
_____
_____
_____
_____

What did God reveal to me about His love?

_____
_____
_____
_____
_____
_____

How can I show myself or others compassion?

_____
_____
_____
_____
_____
_____

Where can God guide me in this area moving forward?

_____
_____
_____
_____
_____
_____

November – Grateful

November - Grateful

Monthly Release

What lies are you ready to stop believing? Write them down here, rip this page out, and GET RID OF THEM!

_____
_____
_____
_____
_____
_____
_____
_____
_____
_____
_____
_____
_____

November - Grateful

November - Grateful

Monthly Declaration

What did the truth of God's word reveal to you?
_____
_____
_____
_____
_____
_____

What scriptures spoke to you the most?
_____
_____
_____
_____
_____
_____

What forgiveness can you give or receive?
_____
_____
_____
_____
_____
_____

What is your prayer this month?
_____
_____
_____
_____
_____
_____

DECEMBER

Beloved

December - Beloved

Prayerful Intentions

As I begin this path on my journey, I pray that:

_____

_____

_____

_____

_____

_____

_____

_____

_____

_____

_____

_____

_____

_____

_____

_____

_____

_____

_____

December - Beloved
Daily Notes

December - Beloved
Daily Notes

December - Beloved
Daily Notes

December - Beloved
Daily Notes

December - Beloved

December - Beloved

Monthly Reflection

How did this theme of Beloved show up in my life this month?

_____
_____
_____
_____
_____
_____

What did God reveal to me about His love?

_____
_____
_____
_____
_____
_____

How can I show myself or others compassion?

_____
_____
_____
_____
_____
_____

Where can God guide me in this area moving forward?

_____
_____
_____
_____
_____
_____

December - Beloved

December – Beloved

Monthly Release

What lies are you ready to stop believing? Write them down here, rip this page out, and GET RID OF THEM!

December - Beloved

December - Beloved

Monthly Declaration

What did the truth of God's word reveal to you?

_____
_____
_____
_____
_____
_____

What scriptures spoke to you the most?

_____
_____
_____
_____
_____
_____

What forgiveness can you give or receive?

_____
_____
_____
_____
_____
_____

What is your prayer this month?

_____
_____
_____
_____
_____
_____

Final Reflection

Looking back to when our journey began, what have you learned along the way?

_____
_____
_____
_____

What did God reveal to you that you want to carry with you always?

_____
_____
_____
_____
_____

Where do you think God is leading you now?

_____
_____
_____
_____

Who could you invite to walk beside you in prayer and support as you continue your journey?

_____
_____
_____
_____
_____

The Journey Continues

As you move forward, I pray you hold tight to everything you discovered on our journey together.

Just look at what God did! Amazing!

God loves you so much and you are absolutely precious, my friend.

Don't you ever forget it!

Love,

Erica